BONE MUSIC

Also by Stephen Cramer

Shiva's Drum

Tongue & Groove

From the Hip

A Little Thyme & a Pinch of Rhyme

Bone Music

Poems by Stephen Cramer

*Winner of the 2015 Louise Bogan Award
for Artistic Merit and Excellence*

Copyright © Stephen Cramer 2016

No part of this book may be used or performed without written consent from the author, if living, except for critical articles or reviews.

Cramer, Stephen
1st edition.

ISBN: 978-0-9965864-1-2
Library of Congress Control Number: 02015915110

Interior Layout by Lea C. Deschenes
Cover Design by Dorinda Wegener
Cover Photo by József Hajdú
Editing by Terry Lucas

Printed in Tennessee, USA
Trio House Press, Inc.
Ponte Vedra Beach, FL

To contact the author, send an email to tayveneese@comcast.net

For Isa, muse extraordinaire

TABLE OF CONTENTS

I

3	Cold was the Ground
7	Giving Blood
11	Sappho
16	Sonnet Ending with a Line by Miles
18	Ming
21	Syrinx
24	Canal & Bridge: Villanelle for Chet Baker

II

29	Passing
33	Haiku for Bud Powell
34	Waterboard
35	Bone Music
38	Price Gun
40	Quarry
43	Canal & Bridge: Villanelle for Chet Baker

III

47	Folk Song Collector
49	Sonnet Ending with a Line by Miles

51	Clerestory
54	Glass
57	Soap
60	Reflex
62	*Tempus Fugit:* Couplets for Stan Getz

IV

67	Rising Sonnet for Miles
68	Chicken
70	Lake Monster
73	Snake Charm Tattoos, Myanmar
76	Bees
78	Falling Pantoum for Art Pepper
80	Witch Doctor
82	Blizzard & Thaw

85	Notes
87	Acknowledgments

I

Cold was the Ground

A moan dragged across
	gravel, a guitar's metallic
complaint & shimmy—

these sounds rattle the zodiac,
	wail to the mute eruption

& flare of a collapsing star. *Dark
	was the Night, Cold
was the Ground*

by Blind Willie Johnson—
	3 minutes & 15 seconds

of bruised spiritual—
	is touring the cosmos
alongside *The Brandenburg*

Concerto & *Johnny
	B. Goode* on the spacecraft

Voyager, the music flanked
	by a slew of natural sounds:
surf & thunder, crickets,

a kiss, a heartbeat—
	an aural primer

to planet Earth. The world
	is phonic. What's matter—
blueberry, backhoe, the back

of your hand—but the shards
       of that primeval sound

when the universe
       detonated from the ghost
of a pebble?

On this journey,
       any *one* man's history

is dwarfed
       by boundless gulf
& pulsar—Voyager,

long past Pluto,
       is 100,000 years

from the next system—
       but here you are
on Earth & so it matters

that when Johnson was 7,
       his stepmother, aiming

for his father, cast lye
       into his face, the price
for his father's infidelity.

Blinded, he was resigned
       to a street corner: the dull

rattle of tips pooling
       in a cup, a woman passing
to another running catalogue

of bouquets—husk of sweat, at first,
        then salt, then almonds—

her body's continuous assertions
        grown hyperbolic. He could
smell moods—their delicate

swerves evident as each
        nuance of skin's pit & swell—

smell the fur
        before it brushed his arm,
before the woman backed away

in a clatter of heels.
        Years later, he could smell

the stench of soaked char
        in the ruined pit
of his house. Turned away

from the hospital after the fire
        that gutted his roof,

he returned to a rain-soaked
        bed of newspaper & soot,
& pneumonia killed him

in the ashes,
        beneath a ceiling

not of wood or plaster
        but of stars.
What are blues

with no human to hear?
....What's a kiss

or a heartbeat
....to that grand sweep
of interplanetary ash

but molecules bumping
....molecules? Stranger, unimaginable

intergalactic pilgrim
....who's never even heard
of a tongue,

if you've found this note
....curled in our million dollar can,

hear the absurdity of our glory
....& our pain. Transmute it
into we know not what:

space dust, star kindling.
....Restore us back to sound.

Giving Blood

The quick pinprick
    opens the smallest
  window in my skin,
the needle tapped
    into my arm to begin

  the long glide
into the surrogate
    vein, liquid poppy
  coiling the tube.

A curtain away,
    a man is absolutely
  delirious, at least

that's how it sounds
    from his protest
  that he don't want
the blood of—
    you fill in the blank:

  a spic, a rag head, a fag—
to pollute his straight, white heart.
    He works up a storm
  of curses, is all

scold & back-talk,
    & heads start to turn
  when he threatens

to jet for the door,
               but instead—
     he's lost his breath—
he collapses
               & I hear the cot

     take his weight.
Even from here,
               my arm cool
     with alcohol,

the artery swollen,
               the pint siphoned off
     to its pouch,

I can tell he's in bad
               shape—I'm thinking car
     accident, more than a brawl—
& before I know it
               part of my life's been

     wheeled away
to be bar-coded,
               refrigerated, then drawn
     into another body

where it'll flood
               muscles & remember
     how to cruise

in its favorite commute—
               the u-turn at fingertip,
     the tug back
to the heart. Repeat.

    Repeat. *Hands off,*
  the man yells. *I wasn't*
dragged into this hole
    to be infected!
  I walked in here

to give away
    the most valuable
  thing I hold,

to spread myself out
    so I'd walk the street
  & wonder if part of me
was with the girl
    on the bench with *angel*

  inked across her shoulders
or maybe the man straddling the Avenue
    swinging his cane like
  he's gonna hit the next cab

out of the park. But for all I know
    my blood'll pulse
  through *this* man's sour tongue,

& for a moment I want
    that bag of my life
  back. Then I recall
how my blood
    isn't my own, how—

  transfusion after transfusion
at birth—I was delivered
    into embrasure,
  a mix of race

   & creed colliding
                 in my cells. So now
         I want that crowd

sluicing inside this man,
              want transfer
       & mixture unending
until—at least in our cells—
               we won't be able

    to tell who's who,
until we're all gliding
               each other's veins.

Sappho

i. In Egypt

Mummified crocodiles—

      her shredded

   songs curved with the dry

       sticks of their tongues.

      Strip by torn
strip, unknowing

       servants applied them

  to the mummy's solemn
ribs, & what ancient

      paste

       could have saved them

   from sifting to trays

of shriveled olives

      & pomegranate

ii. Ellipsis

    Her songs restored, thus:

        unraveled to vacancies,

whole sections traded for
  an arid hush, slender omissions

    abrupting into strains
of a nervous lover—*my tongue*

    breaks up & a delicate fire

  runs through my flesh—
        her body ravished

    by a need so deep

only this forged

        rhythm could keep her

    from breaking down,
   from seeing that the fires

        which rage inside us are a kind

rehearsal for death.
      & how to edge closer

            to that mystery than such

silence

iii. In Lesbos

    Her town market

preserved,

                          its teeming

inventory:
              oyster,

        wine flask, figs

& golden bracelets

        the punctured intervals erasing

              half her city

    so the streets are lent a new,

              imposed syncopation:

    anklebone cups

honey

      chickpeas

        each piece

parceled & perfect,

        as if it were the first time

                            sounds were used

            to signify the world:

crocodile,

        pomegranate,

        the words curving, still wet

                on my tongue.

Sonnet Ending with a Line by Miles

i.

'Trane, of course,
  could start with a phrase & keep

    shattering it until
      he'd been through

every shuffled
  combination,

    until, fracture upon
      fracture, he blew

the phrase from every
  different angle, the run

    collapsing back into itself,
      the quick

transit of his fingertips blurred
  in the sweep

    of those furious
      calisthenics.

The man had truth to play,
    & the truth's

    culmination
        is hard, so he tended

to carry on…
    When he asked his colleague

    Miles ('Trane was still a sideman)
        how to end

a solo, Miles only laughed,
    took a swig,

    & rasped, *you take the damn horn
    out your mouth.*

Ming

        Before the Revolution
ever ruffled a small
corner of the crust—
        but that's the surface

        world, the only place
where redcoats
& rifles make sense…
        Before the Mayflower

        ever drifted with its incidental
human cargo
far above in that land
        of light… Before Galileo spied

        the moons of Jupiter—unimaginable
spheres beyond
the surface's dim
        gleam, beyond leagues & leagues

        of dark until even that murk is pierced
by pinpricks
of shine
        which mean "moons"…

        1602, Ming—the oldest recorded
animal—was born,
& while countries
        rose & fell on land

    eyeless, headless, its daily to-do list
looked something like this:
siphon water, filter
    & waste, & this for 405 years.

    I'd like to say it looks
like some mythical
& striated moth,
    or the ghost of a heart, but really

    the photos are severely
underwhelming
& suggest very little
    beyond their actual subject: two

    halves of a grey quahog clam
propped on a grey
desk. Named
    for the Dynasty during which it was born,

    it burrowed into the bottom dunes
of sands & muck
until it was dredged up
    off the coast of Iceland. Clam shells,

    like trees, sport a new ring
for every year,
& as scientists
    tallied its lifespan—there in the lab—

    it died, which, after the fact,
seems a little
like rewarding
    a marathon's fastest runner

                    by relieving him of his legs.
Some were hoping
this animal
            could buy us the secret

            to longevity. But when we pried it apart,
it only shifted
from one silence
            to another, having ascended

            not into some aquatic afterlife,
dark & briny,
but into our curious heaven,
            into the hands of unmerciful gods.

Syrinx

Meticulously boned apparatus,
trembling chamber,

the membrane taut
but supple as a drum's hide,
its endlessly varied contours

shape avian chatter
to liquid slurs, breezy

chants, a slew
of vocal flourishes
to match the flamboyant

gestures of courting—
strut & wingflash, plume-ruffle,

& the female turning
dully away.   A myth:
Syrinx, an Arcadian nymph,

fled, one day,
through bramble & wood

from a lusting satyr—
& just when—breathless,
unsated—he overtook her,

her prayer of deliverance
was answered
& he reached out to clutch

not her heaving flesh
but an armful of slender

reeds…
Pause of disbelief, exhalation

& astonished echo—
his defeat passing over
the rushes she became,

achieved more than a sigh.
Breath swelled to resonance.

So, story goes, he bound
seven graduated reeds—
a rudimentary scale—

into the pipes
that bear her name.

Syrinx. & let's not pretend
that we've progressed
any further than that satyr,

or even than the fluting
chorus of birds

& their dizzying
courtship.
Because in all our

cawing & crowing
we're still just

calling for mates
& protecting territory,
still just singing

the catalogue of all
we're going to lose.

So let me shape
any crude instrument
I can. Let me breathe

over shaped vacancies.
What else to do

with loss
but build a container
to hold it

then blow it
softly away…

Canal & Bridge: Villanelle for Chet Baker

i.

The opening chords,
          & my window's

     creaking to a gale's sudden
thrust, which somehow blends

          with your horn's shadowy current,
    its darkening pull. I let go

of the album:
          your boyish face chiaroscuroed

    by a streetlamp
as you reach past a lady friend

          & open her car door,
    the wind blowing

what it can of her diminutive skirt. Back then,
          you never had to play a note

    for women to come
running. But *craving*: let's not pretend

          its stormy current, its shadowy pull
    ever let you go.

That last hotel above Amsterdam's
            canals & bridges—you're lost in the afterglow

    & stupor of a couple deep hits, your cheeks
carved into no teeth—& you bend

        toward the open
   window,

lean into
        the drug's crescendo:

   an inner blaze
spangling the lindens,

        the canal's shadow-tossed pull. I wish,
    for once, you could've let go

of your famously relentless
        lust, Chet, but it tugged at you so

    cruelly it was useless
to contend,

        & you opened
   that final window,

faced the current's
        darkening pull, and let go.

II

Passing

Diagonal bands
    of green & gold—
  the man's tie,

lassoed over his hoodie,
    rocks as he rocks

   on an upside-down
bucket on 53rd,
    & the amazing thing

  is not that he's spouting
a continuous log

    of the sidewalk's
  tourist shuffle
but that he doesn't *stop:*

    he's got a rhyme
  for every fabric,

every color & piece
    of clothing
  so he can even include

the woman stepping out
    of the sleek Towncar:

  To the missis in heels,
  you make me feels

*so fine; I think
I feel better than that mink...*

before he segues
         into pleas for cash—

*If you like what I holler
fork over a dollar*

*I take tens, & Honey,
I'll even take a twenty...*

& right now even that
         seems like a bargain
    for a record

of this passing
         day, & I could sit

    for a while watching
this man distill the city
         to clause after non-sequiting

    clause, watching the sentence
shrink to the clouds

         of his breath
    as the conveyor belt
of denim, plaid, corduroy,

         yes, even paisley, continues:

*hey you in the tweed
you got what I need,*

I wish I got paid
like you in the suede

continues till nightfall,
        when most have found
    where they're going,

somewhere warm
        with the properly fluted

    glasses, the right
drinks, & even when sleep
        tries to make him

    call it quits, he's got
one last rhyme:

    Man, life is hard
    without a MasterCard

    I knows it when I sees a
    man with a Visa...

I don't want him
        to stop, don't want to let

    a moment go unrecorded.
So as the rest of us
        get clouded by food

    & drink & talk of the latest
food & drink

        I put my trust in this stranger—
though we're not strangers

to him—& he works out

            another rhyme
     & another, & that city

in the air continues to billow,
            will continue to swell
     & crest & surge as long

as his breath can carry it.

Haiku for Bud Powell

When they left you propped
in the psychiatric ward,

you heard—fingering
the keyboard you sketched

on the wall—not the quiet
tapping of your nails

but the erratic
& shattered swing, the lilt of

Un Poco Loco,
the sound—to your ears—

as sweeping & pervasive
as the fine cement

dusting your fingers,
dusting light switch, bed sheets, your

cheek bones, all that was
left of the song this

dust on all you touched: white blooms
on the barred windowpane...

Waterboard

Sounds like a new ride
at our old amusement

park. Deal of deals:
you don't pay

with tickets, but with silence,
& the less you talk,

the more you ride.

Bone Music

In the 1950s, Russian hipsters found it difficult to get their hands on copies of banned Western music. So they got creative, copying bootleg records onto discarded x-rays.

i.

Inky aquariums, ghost windows:
with vinyl scarce,

we couldn't even bootleg
songs until some back alley genius

first scavenged dumpsters
behind hospitals for this unlikely

savior. The eddy & churn
of snow, gravel underboot,

& then, among syringes
& bandages, beneath battalions

of rubber gloves & masks,
the stashed blessing of discarded x-rays.

ii.

Ah, to bring them home,
  these slides where bodies
are reduced to sooty

maps, cobalt fog inscribed
  with knots of calcium, collagen
streaks. We scissored

each sheet into a circle
  & used the blooming end
of a cigarette to burn

a center hole. Then we pressed
  the contraband of Ellington,
Armstrong, & Basie onto each

until a trumpet's ragged helix
  shimmied on a broken
femur, the cloud

of a skull with its zipper
  of teeth, the stacked
totem of a spine.

iii.

When the state caught
wind, slides grew scarce

as Siberian mangos,
& we scrounged for our own

cat scans, ultrasounds.
Aunt Sofia's MRI

is a Coleman Hawkins,
notes escaping like smoke

from the cage of her ribs.
Bring on winter, bring on

disease, & rot & fracture,
because the more broken

we become, the more music
we can spin out of our bones.

Price Gun

Not the usual
stick-up routine

on my way back
from the market, a bag

of bread, cheese, cold
plums. Someone must've swiped

a price-gun, & so
for three long

Harlem blocks
it was lamp post: 50 cents,

hydrant: $2.40, a string
of car windows going

for a quarter a piece.
Yard sale

without the yard,
there, finally, was proof:

who says you can't
put a price on the world

says wrong. All the way home,
I looked for the culprit,

a slight swagger
in his step

because for an entire
afternoon—until, at least,

next rain—
it looked like that whole

unattainable city
was up for grabs.

Quarry

We tested grip & muscle
      against the cliff's crumbling vertical,
           dislodging fist-sized clumps

of clay from time
      & pressure: a ridged shield

      grafted to stone,
some animal's protection
      long surviving the soft

      flesh it was charged to protect,
the dim chatter of the creek behind

      turning to the rasp & gurgle
           this creature once made
trawling shallow seas, the click

      of molting that left this husk
           to the clutch of sand & 250

million years. Hard
      to say, standing at the foot
           of that cliff, which is more

difficult—reinventing an age
      that long gone or conjuring one

           that far in the future: years
after the glaciers' long march
      south, after the gorges have been carved

             through our cities, our proudest
monuments scraped to gravel

        so a few scraps of apartment buildings
                are left staring at a canyon, the newest
& broadest Broadway in town,

        we—with all our wise engineering—
                will have become the good

calcium streaking a crag, the residual iron
        forgetting the blood
                that drove it. Who knows

how many times
        we've already looked

                into the eyes of those
whose ancestors will replace us,
        the muzzle that'll drag

                from the dirt an arc of petrified
teeth or a human femur.

        The day the trilobite
                could no longer keep up
with the terrain gone protean

        around it, did some part
                of its slight skeleton know it?

Back to the car, I click
        myself in, shift into gear,
                & accelerate down the road

we've blasted through rock,
  past the geometry of fields

    with trimmed & tidy crops
that won't outlast us by a decade.
  I ease my foot onto the pedal

    to release into the engine
just enough of the liquid
  that's helping to drive us toward

    this future—& I'm just
a shade looking on
  at a world of shades.

Canal & Bridge: Villanelle for Chet Baker

ii.

We whirled
                      to your groove—

       eyes closed, arms
spread, spurred

             on by your breath,
    & you almost blew

our bodies into a tremor of morning
               glories. Chet, you've

      fused mirth & burn,
blurred

            the world to one
    continuous groove,

yours, & it simmers
            & moves

     so fluidly there's no way
to put into words

             your breathy,
      almost blue

gush & swell. You play
             like you're out to prove

       that your hurt
& minor thirds

              can whirl
       to a single groove.

Pausing between
              phrases, you remove

       the mouthpiece, empty spit
&, undeterred,

              resume your breath
       to an almost blue

drizzle of notes. I open
              my eyes. I remove

       the needle, flip
the side, & the record

              whirls into
    its groove:

one deep breath,
              then *Almost Blue*...

III

Folk Song Collector

Languages stolen
from the tongue
morph into a yodel's

minor tremolo & forget
their own meaning,
so there's no remedy

for my fingers' itch
to click the cassette
home. I'm drawn

by rumor to a woman
with the memory
of work songs

stowed in her chest—
song that says *lace
the needle through,*

song that says
*brace the wrist
to pound grain to flour.*

Dusk's insinuation
over rampant loosestrife
& briar, the cabin squat

against the ridge,
& she opens
her mouth to a hymn

that's a mix of cicada
& train whistle,
jewelweed & honeysuckle.

Ambushed
by the future,
she doesn't understand

when she hears herself
played back,
the mechanics

of pause & rewind,
&: *never done thought
I'd live to see my voice*

*spun up, looped
round & round.*

Sonnet Ending with a Line by Miles

ii.

Hackensack,
    October '56:

        van Gelder, in the control booth,
            looked down,

asked the name of the tune—
    a fair question—

        but because Miles knew
            that if you're too quick

to name it, you can smother
    the mystery,

        he stopped, & before
            snapping off the countdown

to Jo Jones who twice hit
    the high-hat

        like a train
            pulling out of the station,

unreeled a simple skein
    of ten words that

        meant *hey, sit tight*
            & observe history.

The title? Not even he
    dared say it—

    we're talking Miles,
        the song's creator.

Just before
    he put horn to lips: *I'll play it,*

    said Miles,
        & tell you what it is later.

Clerestory

5th Ave's fierce intermingling—
jostle & surge
of selfhood, each of us

a fraction of rush hour's
1,000-footed god.

Such anonymous
intimacy, the way
we're thrust against

another's skin,
& I'm as good

as lashed to a man
tattooed wrist to wrist
with an eclectic

collage: no anchor
or arrow-pierced

heart, but flames sprouting
wings, a swatch of roiled
clouds, a strange

triumvirate of hammer,
saw & candle. No one

would dare try to thieve
this anarchic lot
but just in case,

he's flanked himself
with wreaths of coiled

thorn & barb–
such vigorous barricades
that he's more ink

than skin. Leather
tanktop & tassled boots,

you might expect this man
abruptly to sidestep
into a bar or to straddle

a wide Harley & thunder
through traffic.

But instead, 50th street,
he strides up
to the cathedral

& steps inside
to stained glass'

shower of filament
& splinter. Burning
bush & tablet, staff

& cleft rosettes,
the windows' tiered narratives

play themselves out
on passersby,
people's flesh alive

with ancient verbs.
You & I leave,

& we're stripped
of light, become again
our daily selves,

but when this man
steps out those doors,

he takes his stories
with him. Hammer,
saw & candle—

embodiment, let's guess,
of redemption through

work. Imagine
if all our flesh framed
what drove us—the urgent,

the consequential. Look
at my skin, its opaque

& revelatory panes.
This birthmark
denotes good fortune,

this slash
where I've been burned.

Glass

Windshields blast to the curb
        when a single mortar wastes
                every window for
blocks, a storefront pane

        shattered & swept away
                so pigeons swagger

on what's left of the tabouleh
        & canned chickpeas
                inside. Months ago, dozens
of men trailed Omar al-Ibrahim,

        a glass salesman,
                like his van held The Answer

& not just sheet after sheet
        of glass packed like file folders
                on the padded floor.
This week, his tape measure

        splayed with garlands of Arabic,
                he sizes up just a single

splintered pane: the bay
        window of a battered house.
                With paint unraveling to ashen corkscrews,
he & his partner work their slow

        repair—shatter what's left,
                fit the new. *Around here,*

he says, *glass sales*
    can gauge morale better
        than any of your news polls.
High sales reveal confidence,

    at least a shred of hope. Low—
        he pauses—*well, people learn*

not to replace
    a bedroom pane when every night
        bullets pock the concrete.
When work is done, the pane

    on the young Iraqi's house
        is the only part that doesn't look

like it's about to cave in.
    I just stumbled into this life,
        the owner means by this repair. *The bus*
took a wrong turn, & when I stepped off,

    my neighborhood turned rife with foxhole
        & bunker. Now the man stands

beside a vase with one incongruous
    orange flower, glancing out
        his new window as though nothing
came between him

    & the reckless world. *Trust*
        is like that, Mr. al-Ibrahim says:
you can't see it, but you know
    when it's gone. As his van
        backs out to the street,

shards glint from the gutters,

    & long before they're washed
        into the murk of the Euphrates,

caravans of Humvees crush them
    under their wheels, & they're ground
        & ground to an incongruous
new version of desert sand, into this

    dazzling blue dust.

Soap

No dramatization
        necessary: we've already seen
the kick-down-the-door
        routine, the lights

blitzing-the-eyes routine,
        the routine of questioning,
the show of courtesy
        before the charge

up the stairs routine,
        the procedure that leaves eight
dead, a single woman
        on her knees

& the uniforms clomping back out
        to ambush the street…
& now, on the news, the ticker
        reads *sedition* because a senator

spoke out against what they called
        a *routine raid*, what was really
an *assault* made lawful
        because that country's ground

was rich with oil.
        Won't this senator
keep his mouth shut
        like a good citizen? The dissenting

Russian poet, imprisoned in the 80's—
        years without pencil or paper—
was supposed to be silenced.
        But she scratched her protest

with a burnt match
        into a bar of soap
& repeated those phrases
        to herself till they thumped

with the thump of blood
        through her wrists.
Then, with a single rinse,
        she rubbed the words

on the nape of her neck
        & elbow crease—yes,
to rid herself of the labor
        camp's fleas & lice

but mostly to erase the crime
        of her thought, the words
dissolving to liquid
        glimmer as they twisted

in the filthy drain…
        So, Senator, welcome to prison,
where our voices are banned,
        where we continue to carve out

word after outlawed word, even if
        their audience is a plank of soap,
a match & the walls,
        where the guards

in suits and ties smirk
        as the stream of endless drain water
cleanses us from above
        as we rinse from our bodies

the lather & froth
        of all we can't say.

Reflex

You shake your hips
        & Tired buys orange

running shoes to do laps
        around my chest

Sobriety guzzles
        Robitussin & rubbing

alcohol on the rocks
        & passes out on the floor

we touch & Responsible
        quits his job

& jumps out the window
        Boredom breaks out

the hoola hoops
        we kiss & Dirty

showers,
        throws on a tux

& knits a tie
        Stability drops

out of school & works
        the circus trapeze

oh me
        oh my, my honey tree,

my sweets, Heavy
      packs all its trunks with lead

& floats away

Tempus Fugit:
Couplets for Stan Getz

The 16 inch slash
        from his left nipple

around to his backbone
           wouldn't cripple

his style, but
        having his chest muscles cut,

his ribs pried apart
           so surgeons could root

through artery & bone: that might.
        Still, they collapsed

his lung, steered toward
           the fist-sized tumor trapped

between his heart
        & spine…*Dis here*

finado, he liked to say
           that year,

though it *wasn't* over,
        not quite: his side

sewn up, his muscles
           relearning how to bind

& flex... No stitch could hope
        to withhold the manic

grind of *Tempus Fugit*,
           the frantic

laddering of sixteenths,
        but what can you say

when you hear those last
            records: the way

every fluid & bottomless
        run he blows

tests the seams
           of those restrung sinews,

some notes amplified,
        while others are muffled, caught

in the hole
           between his spine & heart.

IV

Rising Sonnet for Miles

St. Louis, '44: Miles was 18,
fresh out of high school, & seeing Bird

& Diz on one stage was a daydream
to rival his most carnal. When he heard

those escalating exchanges, the opposite
of gravity, it was like the first time

he rode an elevator: when Diz hit
floor three, Miles' heart filled his shoes. As they climbed,

he imagined smashing through the ceiling
to cruise among stars beyond the Milky Way,

that spill of pearls below. *The greatest feeling
I ever had in my life,* he'd say,

then, with a smirk, *with my clothes on,* that is—
St. Louis, '44: Bird and Diz.

Chicken

At the harvest festival
when we were celebrating
with pumpkin tarts
& cider, an older farmer
asked what I was *into*
& maybe my answer
was muffled a bit
from the cider's tang
because he started
talking passionately
not about his favorite poet
or the use of weather in haiku
but about his chickens:
White Leghorns, Silkie
Bantams, Rhode Island
Reds, Buff Orpingtons,
how, in Corporate Agriculture
the birds are bred so big
that their legs
cripple beneath them
& isn't that a shame.
I tried to break in,
to tell him he misheard.
But he shook his head
& held up his finger.
That's not the case with *his* birds.
When *his* hens are laying
he puts oyster shells
in their grit
to give them extra
calcium for their own shells.
His birds are free range—

not de-beaked
& stuffed two dozen
to a pen. Freedom
makes all the difference
in the world. You can *taste*
their happiness, he said,
even *see* it—
their yolks a rich,
almost tangerine color,
not pale like those
you get from the grocery,
& he was starting to get
short of breath
from excitement,
& by this time,
to tell the truth,
I was just hoping
he didn't ask
about my birds
because I don't know
if I could've broken it
to him: *poetry,*
I said, *not poultry.*

Lake Monster

When the shore's sleek curve,
this morning, steers me
toward the bay

where sun-glare warps the water's
shadow-heave & lurch

into scaled musculature,
I know it should be
just a wind slick,

or boat wake,
drift wood gnarled

into a craning
neck or a cormorant
caught from behind.

I know how
far off glint & shadow

can be bent to fit
conjecture. But suddenly
I've entered the arena

of hoax & tabloid, home
video & grainy

photo—shadows tampered
to the arch of a back,
the slick of wet

scales, the negatives
lost. Proof's elusive,

though that doesn't stop
people head-lamped at midnight,
timing their search

to the rise of shoals
with the moon

or scientists whose mics
pick up stuttered ticks
& chirps akin to beluga

whales. *Believe,*
a bumper sticker advises,

though skeptics are quick
to point out we've found
no teeth or bones,

that a population so small
couldn't sustain itself.

Still, as we always do, I crave
the elusive. So I squint
into the murk

for a glimmer that flows
& glides. All we can do

is praise those veering wavelets
that tease the edge
of our sight.

All we can do
is seek those shadows

that turn when we turn,
& will never reveal themselves
or fully disappear.

Snake Charm Tattoos, Myanmar

The ink, cut with venom,
        cleaves to florettes
as a tribe member

        siphons the mixture
with a needle
        to spur his neighbor's
already-indigoed flesh.

        This clan of urban
snake-wranglers
        circles up for their weekly

        tattooing, the touching up
of charms
        so when they hand-capture
their quarry & free them

in the outskirts,
        poison is voided
by their blood's new

        resistance.
They will not kill,
        though that ensures
that heaps of snakes

will sidle their way
        back to town's
sun-baked gutters

           dozens, sometimes hundreds of times…
One pre-school noon,
           when two of us
almost stumbled on a coil

of rope that focused
           into the shock
of a snake's

           reluctant unspooling,
the teachers didn't
           usher it to deeper
woods. They herded us away,

but not so far away
           that we missed the gleam
of the shovel, the crunch

           of bone & dirt. After that stark
initiation into our habit
           of expulsion,
we'd soon grow

into the endless figure-eights
           of all we buy
to purify hearth

           & heart. So, my serpentine brothers,
forgive me my late conversion
           as I'm inked into this tribe.
Let someone dole out

a dose of poison—
           if that's what it takes—
to spur & prick me

   into a larger embrasure.
I want to touch
   what I fear. I want to be left
scarred & charmed.

Bees

My father is striding up the stairs
of the deck he built
two at a time. From inside

the screen door,
I see the mob—spiked
swarm of brushfire—

before he does
& wave at him
to go back.

He comes anyway.
He's got good news.
He's always got

good news. Then,
when they strike—
this is the part

I'm seeing again
& again this morning—
he takes them

into his mouth,
every last one,
wild & fuming. The air

is sucked of its droning.
The wind in the trees
is gone, & I can't move.

Then, with one fluid
exhalation,
he blows the bees back out,

& I madly tug
the door open.
Did they sting you? I ask,

& he answers, slowly,
with a swollen tongue,
tastes like honey.

Falling Pantoum for Art Pepper

Cursing God, we couldn't even
        find the *door*
after Dianne dropped
        all the bottles

to a crystalline maze of capsule dust
        & shattered glass:
dull gems of deep burn, the endless
        refrain of sifting shards for pills…

Those damn splintered
        bottles
meant four days
        of sliced fingers,

dulled nerve ends. How to break
        this refrain of shards & pills?
I swear: if she could've gotten
        out of the house,

slicking the knob
        with gashed fingers,
she'd have searched out
        the beams of a bridge.

But there was no *way*
        we were getting out,
& in our panic we kept
        falling to bloody palms,

the search delirious…
        I can see our leap from a bridge,
lost t-shirts
            twirling lazily above us:

the crazy rush of falling,
        our blood oddly calm
as we turn pure sound:
            a scale descending to silence,

an unleashed hurt
        swirling away from us,
the air shattering us
        like glass…

Man, we would've turned pure
        sound, descended to that final applause
of water, but I swear to God,
            we couldn't find the door.

Witch Doctor

She may not got
much teeth, but
if she likes you

she'll make
your skinniest hen
lay a double-yolked

egg. I knocked
on her door,
still learning to shed

all my muscles
had acquired:
the rigidity of curb,

my step aligned
to the obedience
of crosswalk & yield.

She mixed herself
a bowl of yolk
& ashes—the sticky

pulp of birth
& departure—slicked
her hands with it,

& darkened her body
with a second skin,
exhaling incantations,

slipping in & out
of two languages
like a high heel

& a clog. A breeze
lifted from the lake,
& as she washed,

& tempera dissolved
to the water basin's
wood, she sang

her dream:
the snake's
scaled rainbow

coiling the grass
as it tunneled
out of itself,

the clouded membrane
finally torn
from its eyes.

Blizzard & Thaw

Asterisk &
      spoked plumage,

  mandala

        of needled

   glint & dendrite

they all swivel
        & wheel

   on a spindle

       of air to land

on a black tray
   held by a farmer
  all but washed out

          by blue drifts
  years before
    the blizzard

that invaded
   his lungs

       until it raged

  their shallow
    billows to a stop

he bends
      to parcel & inventory
  the storm:

     pearly fern
  spangle & rosette
        & gingerly

lifts them
  to a microscope's slide

      fragments brushed off

with a turkey

       feather
   & he wheels them

  into focus

& clicks
      the photo
    just before

they evaporate
    & he inhales them
  & they're fused

       into the heat

  at the back
    of his throat

     not pulverized
  or shattered

but consumed

                        into anonymity

        the way we rush

                            toward gone

Notes

"Cold was the Ground" is for David Wojahn, whose poem "Homage to Blind Willie Johnson" triggered this one.

"Sappho": Almost two and a half thousand years after she lived, papyrus rolls scrawled with her poems were discovered in Egypt. They had been used not only as wrappings for mummies but also balled up and stuffed into the carcasses of sacred animals.

"Ming" is for Bob "The Hawk" Heiser, who first brought this story—among many others—to my attention.

"Syrinx" is for Alejandro.

"Canal & Bridge: Villanelle for Chet Baker" is for Mark Doty and Lynda Hull, whose poems ("Almost Blue," and "Lost Fugue for Chet," respectively) inspired these.

"Haiku For Bud Powell": In 1974, Bud Powell, the great bebop pianist, was admitted to Creedmoor Psychiatric Center, where he stayed for over a year.

"Sonnet Ending with Lines by Miles, section 2": Rudy Van Gelder was the recording engineer for this session.

"Soap": In the early 1980s, Irena Ratushinskaya was charged by the Soviet government with "the dissemination of slanderous documentation in poetic form." She received a seven-year sentence to labor camp, where she continued, in secret, to write poetry on bars of soap.

"*Tempus Fugit*: Couplets for Stan Getz": This story is lifted from a paragraph late in *Stan Getz, a Life in Jazz*, by Donald L. Maggin.

"Chicken" is for Bok Choy, Colonel Bokkers, and Mrs. Fluffington.

"Snake Charm Tattoos, Myanmar" is for Scott Hightower.

"Falling Pantoum for Art Pepper": Some of the details in this poem are taken from Pepper's autobiography, *Straight Life*.

"Blizzard & Thaw" is for Mike B because he kinda likes snow. Snowflake Bentley lived in Jericho, Vermont, from 1865-1931. He was the first person to photograph a single snowflake at a time.

Acknowledgments

Grateful acknowledgement is made to the following journals in which these poems appeared, sometimes in earlier versions:

African American Review: "Sonnets Ending with a Line by Miles," section 1

The American Poetry Review: "Ming"

Barrow Street: "Price Gun"

Brilliant Corners: "Canal & Bridge: Villanelle for Chet Baker," section 2 and "Sonnets Ending with a Line by Miles," section 2

Fogged Clarity: "Rising Sonnet for Miles" and "*Tempus Fugit*: Couplets for Stan Getz"

Gihon River Review: "Folk Song Collector"

Green Mountains Review: "Cold was the Ground" and "Haiku for Bud Powell"

Harvard Review: "Passing"

The Literary Review: "Clerestory"

New Ohio Review: "Chicken"

Ocean State Review: "Lake Monster"

Pamplemousse: "Reflex"

The Salon: "Snake Charm Tattoos, Myanmar"

Statorec.com: "Sappho" and "Witch Doctor"

Vantage Point: "Canal & Bridge: Villanelle for Chet Baker," section 1

The Worcester Review: "Waterboard"

I am also grateful for the support of the Vermont Arts Council, a grant from which greatly assisted the writing of this book. And lastly, I owe many thanks to the whole team at Trio House Press, especially Terry Lucas, whose sharp eye catches all.

About the Author

Stephen Cramer's first book of poems, *Shiva's Drum*, was selected for the National Poetry Series and published by University of Illinois Press. His second, *Tongue & Groove*, was also published by University of Illinois. *From the Hip*, which follows the history of hip hop in a series of 56 sonnets, and *A Little Thyme & A Pinch of Rhyme*, a cookbook in haiku and sonnets, came out from Wind Ridge Press in 2014 and 2015. His work has appeared in journals such as *The American Poetry Review, African American Review, The Yale Review, Harvard Review,* and *Hayden's Ferry Review*. An Assistant Poetry Editor at *Green Mountains Review*, he teaches writing and literature at the University of Vermont and lives with his wife and daughter in Burlington.

About the Artist

József Hajdú is a Hungarian photographer represented by the Bolt Photo Gallery of Contemporary Arts in Budapest.

About the Book

Bone Music was designed at Trio House Press through the collaboration of:

Terry Lucas, Lead Editor
József Hajdú, Cover Photo
Dorinda Wegener, Cover Design
Lea Deschenes, Interior Design

The text is set in Adobe Caslon Pro.

The publication of this book is made possible, whole or in part, by the generous support of the following individuals and/or agencies:

Anonymous

About the Press

Trio House Press is a collective press. Individuals within our organization come together and are motivated by the primary shared goal of publishing distinct American voices in poetry. All THP published poets must agree to serve as Collective Members of the Trio House Press for twenty-four months after publication in order to assist with the press and bring more Trio books into print. Award winners and published poets must serve on one of four committees: Production and Design, Distribution and Sales, Educational Development, or Fundraising and Marketing. Our Collective Members reside in cities from New York to San Francisco.

Trio House Press adheres to and supports all ethical standards and guidelines outlined by the CLMP.

The Editors of Trio House Press would like to thank Kimiko Hahn.

Trio House Press, Inc. is dedicated to the promotion of poetry as literary art, which enhances the human experience and its culture. We contribute in an innovative and distinct way to American Poetry by publishing emerging and established poets, providing educational materials, and fostering the artistic process of writing poetry. For further information, or to consider making a donation to Trio House Press, please visit us online at: www.triohousepress.org.

Other Trio House Press Books you might enjoy:

Rigging a Chevy into a Time Machine and Other Ways to Escape a Plague by Carolyn Hembree
    2015 Trio Award Winner selected by Neil Shepard

Magpies in the Valley of Oleanders by Kyle McCord, 2015

Your Immaculate Heart by Annmarie O'Connell, 2015

The Alchemy of My Mortal Form by Sandy Longhorn
    2014 Louise Bogan Winner selected by Carol Frost

What the Night Numbered by Bradford Tice
    2014 Trio Award Winner selected by Peter Campion

Flight of August by Lawrence Eby
    2013 Louise Bogan Winner selected by Joan Houlihan

The Consolations by John W. Evans
    2013 Trio Award Winner selected by Mihaela Moscaliuc

Fellow Odd Fellow by Steven Riel, 2013

Clay by David Groff
    2012 Louise Bogan Winner selected by Michael Waters

Gold Passage by Iris Jamahl Dunkle
    2012 Trio Award Winner selected by Ross Gay

If You're Lucky Is a Theory of Mine by Matt Mauch, 2012

www.ingramcontent.com/pod-product-compliance
Lightning Source LLC
Chambersburg PA
CBHW020621300426
44113CB00007B/730